Military and Security Developments Involving the Democratic People's Republic of Korea 2013

A Report to Congress

Pursuant to the National Defense Authorization Act for Fiscal Year 2012

Section 1236 of the National Defense Authorization Act for Fiscal Year 2012, Public Law 112-81, as amended by Section 1292 of the National Defense Authorization Act for Fiscal Year 2013, provides that the Secretary of Defense shall submit a report "in both classified and unclassified form, on the current and future military power of the Democratic People's Republic of Korea" (DPRK). The report shall address an assessment of the security situation on the Korean Peninsula, the goals and factors shaping North Korean security strategy and military strategy, trends in North Korean security, an assessment of North Korea's regional security objectives, including an assessment of the North Korean military's capabilities, developments in North Korean military doctrine and training, an assessment of North Korea's proliferation activities, and other military security developments.

(This page intentionally left blank)

Table of Contents

(This page intentionally left blank)

EXECUTIVE SUMMARY

The Democratic People's Republic of Korea (DPRK) remains one of the United States' most critical security challenges for many reasons. These include North Korea's willingness to undertake provocative and destabilizing behavior, including attacks on the Republic of Korea (ROK), its pursuit of nuclear weapons and long-range ballistic missiles, and its willingness to proliferate weapons in contravention of United Nations Security Council Resolutions.

Under Kim Jong Il, DPRK strategy focused on internal security; coercive diplomacy to compel acceptance of its diplomatic, economic, and security interests; development of strategic military capabilities to deter external attack; and challenging the ROK and the U.S.-ROK Alliance. We anticipate these strategic goals will be consistent under North Korea's current leader, Kim Jong Un.

North Korea fields a large, forward-deployed military that retains the capability to inflict serious damage on the ROK, despite significant resource shortfalls and aging hardware. The DPRK continues to be deterred from conducting large-scale attacks on the ROK primarily due to the strength of the U.S.-ROK Alliance. On a smaller scale, however, the DPRK has demonstrated its willingness to use military provocation to achieve national goals. In 2010, it sank the ROK naval vessel *CHEONAN,* killing 46 ROK Navy sailors, and shelled Yeonpyeong Island, killing two ROK Marines and two civilians.

North Korea's continued pursuit of nuclear technology and capabilities and development of intermediate- and long-range ballistic missile programs, as reflected in the December 2012 Taepo Dong-2 missile launch and February 2013 nuclear test, underscore the threat to regional stability and U.S. national security posed by North Korea. These programs, and North Korea's expressed hostility toward the ROK and proliferation of items prohibited under United Nations Security Council Resolutions 1718, 1874, 2087,and 2094, make the DPRK a continued security challenge for the United States and its Allies and partners.

North Korea's third nuclear test in February 2013 and subsequent announcement of plans to restart and refurbish nuclear facilities at Yongbyon highlight the continued challenge posed by its nuclear programs. The September 19, 2005 Joint Statement of the Six-Party Talks, and United Nations Security Council Resolutions 1718, 1874, 2087, and 2094 call for the complete and verifiable denuclearization of North Korea. Given North Korea's unwillingness to abide by these commitments, the U.S. Department of Defense will continue to manage the North Korean security challenge through close coordination and consultation with the international community, particularly with our ROK and Japanese Allies.

The United States remains vigilant in the face of North Korea's continued provocations and steadfast in its commitments to Allies in the region, including the security provided by extended deterrence commitments through the nuclear umbrella and conventional forces.

CHAPTER ONE:
ASSESSMENT OF THE SECURITY SITUATION

KEY DEVELOPMENTS IN NORTH KOREAN AND PENINSULAR SECURITY

In the past year, the Democratic People's Republic of Korea (DPRK or North Korea) ended its institutional readjustment to Kim Jong Un's leadership and began implementation of his broader national agenda. Much like his father, Kim Jong Un has adopted a strategy of using coercive acts—force or the threat of force—to influence adversaries and achieve policy objectives. At the beginning of his second year in power, Kim sought to use another coercive campaign to advance the longstanding goals of gaining international recognition and de facto acceptance as a nuclear state. The December 2012 launch of the Taepo Dong-2 (TD-2) intercontinental ballistic missile (ICBM)/space launch vehicle (SLV) led to a series of actions that included a nuclear test in February 2013 and public threats to strike the U.S. mainland with nuclear weapons. The North also declared itself unbound from core diplomatic agreements, such as the 1953 Korean War Armistice Agreement.

In April 2013, after declaring it would no longer pursue denuclearization, the regime announced it would begin a "new strategic line" of simultaneous nuclear weapons development and economic improvement. By late May, the regime began a campaign of diplomatic outreach to mitigate the long-term political and economic damage of its actions. North Korea began appeals to the international community for restored dialogue, and dispatched high-level envoys to China and Russia. By mid-summer, North Korea accepted South Korean preconditions to resume operations at the Kaesong Industrial Complex, after North Korea withdrew its workers from the project in April 2013.

As of October, North Korea continued to repeat publicly that it was open to resuming dialogue with the United States and the region, but it was unlikely to make significant concessions on relinquishing its nuclear program. Its earlier campaign of diplomatic outreach was tempered by its September cancellation of inter-Korean reunions and its bellicose rhetoric, including statements defaming ROK President Park Geun-hye. North Korea's stated intent to advance its nuclear program and continue ballistic missile/space launch vehicle efforts implies that it will eventually return to coercive actions to achieve its goals in the future.

NORTH KOREAN SECURITY PERCEPTIONS

North Korean threat perceptions are shaped by many factors. These include a legacy of guerilla warfare dating back to its anti-colonial struggle against the Japanese, political and economic isolation, experience eliminating internal threats to the Kim family, and a political culture that is defined by an unending existential struggle with outside forces.

The regime sees threats emanating from inside and outside the country. It does not fully trust regional actors, including its supposed allies China and Russia, nor does it trust its own population. The regime continues to portray a garrison state worldview of imminent threat, which serves to justify draconian internal security controls, vast expenditures on the military, and continued rule by the Kim family as the sole protectors of the state.

Internally, the Kim regime remains concerned with ideological control of its citizenry, which has grown increasingly less reliant on the state for basic goods and services. In the absence of large-scale economic improvement, the regime continues to prioritize ideological indoctrination, intimidation, and preferential treatment of the privileged elite in Pyongyang and of select military units.

The Recent Purge of Chang Song-taek

Kim Jong Un's decision in December 2013 to purge and execute his powerful uncle, Chang Song-taek, is unlikely to lead to major changes in defense policy or internal stability in the near-term. Chang was a four-star General and vice-chairman of the National Defense Commission yet had little formal control over defense and military portfolios. His absence will most likely be felt in the economy, as Chang was in charge of several high-profile initiatives, particularly with China, to attract foreign currency and investment to North Korea.

Chang was believed to be a relatively pragmatic advisor to Kim Jong Un, but his influence probably waned in 2013. Chang's public appearances with his nephew, which is used to signal an individual's importance within the regime, dropped 50 percent in 2013 compared to 2012. Chang's execution is the most significant step to date in Kim's establishment of his authority, eliminating arguably the most influential senior Party official remaining from his father's era. The sudden and brutal purge sends a strong message to regime elites that the formation of factions or potential challenges to Kim Jong Un will not be tolerated.

CHAPTER TWO:
UNDERSTANDING NORTH KOREA'S STRATEGY

STRATEGIC GOALS

North Korean goals and strategies reflect the reality of political isolation, significant economic deprivation, deterioration of its conventional military, and increasing political, economic, and military power of nearby states. The strategic goal of the regime is to ensure the survival of the Kim dynasty and ideological control over the North Korean population in perpetuity. The overarching national security objectives to achieve this goal under Kim Jong Un have not changed markedly from those pursued by Kim Jong Il: international recognition as a nuclear-armed state, maintenance of a viable deterrent capability, and reunification of Korea under North Korea's control. The North continues to use reunification with the South as a key component of its national identity narrative, to validate its strategy and policies, and to justify sacrifices demanded of the populace. However, North Korea's leaders almost certainly recognize that achieving this objective is, for the foreseeable future, unattainable.

NATIONAL STRATEGY

Beyond its fundamental role as a guarantor of national and regime security, the North Korean military supports the Kim regime's use of coercive diplomacy as part of its larger diplomatic strategy. North Korea uses limited provocations—even those that are kinetic and lethal in nature—such as military actions and small-scale attacks to gain psychological advantage in diplomacy and win limited political and economic concessions, all while likely believing it can control escalation.

Closely tied to this strategy of political coercion are North Korea's nuclear and ballistic missile programs. DPRK leaders see these programs, absent normalized relations with the international community, as leading to a credible deterrence capability essential to its goals of survival, sovereignty, and relevance and supportive of its coercive military threats and actions.

REGIONAL OBJECTIVES AND BEHAVIOR

North Korea remains focused on extracting economic aid and diplomatic concessions from regional nations while defending against threats to its sovereignty. In 2013, North Korea increased diplomatic overtures to regional states but such outreach failed to produce meaningful political gains because of international concerns about its nuclear weapons program. The North likely believes a "charm offensive" will eventually lead to improvements in regional relationships and gradual advancement of its strategic objectives.

The temporary thaw in inter-Korean relations over the summer of 2013 came to a stand-still when North Korea cancelled inter-Korean family reunions just four days before their scheduled late-September start. Although North Korea has pressed for a resumption of tourism on Mount Kumgang, a potential source of revenue for North Korea, the ROK is unwilling to begin discussions absent progress on family reunions. Despite these setbacks, the ROK shows no signs of abandoning the Park Administration's trustpolitik policy and remains steadfast in insisting that a return to Six-Party Talks be predicated on North Korea demonstrating its serious commitment to denuclearization.

North Korea remains dependent on China as a key diplomatic and economic benefactor, and North Korea is conscious of China's anger at its actions as it seeks to advance its nuclear and missile capabilities. Although the North Korean regime is aware that China disapproves of its nuclear program and use of coercive actions, the regime likely thinks China is primarily interested in preserving regional stability and will refrain from punishing North Korea too severely or cutting off diplomatic or economic ties.

North Korea also maintains friendly relations with Russia, though the relationship is less robust than North Korea's relationship with China. In September, Russia opened a new rail link into North Korea. During a November summit with South Korean President Park, President Putin signed a memorandum of understanding encouraging ROK private sector investment in the rail link. Long-stalled plans for the creation of a natural gas pipeline from Russia to South Korea through North Korea – a project that could earn North Korea millions of dollars annually in transit fees – have made little concrete progress in recent years. The North remains willing to disrupt relations with regional neighbors temporarily and absorb the associated cost when it believes coercive actions toward South Korea or the United States will advance its strategic objectives.

North Korean relations with Japan thawed somewhat in 2013. In May, the North accepted a visit by a Japanese delegation and indicated it might be willing to discuss the longstanding issue of Japanese citizens abducted by North Korea in the 1970s and 1980s. To date, no further progress has been made on this issue.

CHAPTER THREE:
FORCE MODERNIZATION GOALS AND TRENDS

OVERVIEW

North Korea's large, forward-positioned military can initiate an attack against the ROK with little or no warning, even though it suffers from resource shortages and aging equipment. The military retains the capability to inflict significant damage on the ROK, especially in the region from the demilitarized zone (DMZ) to Seoul. Although North Korea is unlikely to attack on a scale it assesses would risk its survival by inviting overwhelming counterattacks by the ROK and the United States, North Korea's calculus of the threshold for smaller, asymmetric attacks and provocations is unclear. North Korea's special operations forces (SOF), artillery, and growing missile force provide significant capabilities for small-scale attacks that could rapidly spiral into a larger conflict.

North Korea is making some efforts to upgrade its large arsenal of mostly outdated conventional weapons. It has reinforced long-range artillery forces near the DMZ and has a substantial number of mobile ballistic missiles that could strike a variety of targets in the ROK and Japan. However, the DPRK's emphasis will likely be on defensive and asymmetric attack capabilities, and it will attempt to leverage the perception of a nuclear deterrent to counter technologically superior ROK and U.S. conventional forces.

North Korea will seek to continue to develop and test-launch missiles, including the TD-2 ICBM/SLV. Missile tests and programs to improve denial and deception, electronic warfare, road-mobile ICBM development, and SOF, are driven by North Korea's desire to enhance deterrence and defense, and to improve its ability to conduct limited attacks against the South.

MAINTAINING THE THREAT

Although it faces many internal challenges and constraints, including deterioration of its conventional capabilities, the North Korean military poses a serious threat to the ROK, its other neighbors, and U.S. forces in the region.

Amid a period of heightened tensions In March, North Korean media highlighted Kim Jong Un's approval of the Strategic Rocket Force's (SRF) "firepower strike plan" at an emergency operations meeting. The report included photographs of Kim Jong Un reviewing maps purportedly showing intercontinental strike plans—likely aspirational—against the United States.

AN AGING FORCE...

The Korean People's Army (KPA)—an umbrella organization comprising ground, air, naval, missile, and SOF—ranks in personnel numbers as the fourth largest military in the world. Four to five percent of North Korea's 24 million people serve on active duty, and another 25 to 30 percent is assigned to a reserve or paramilitary unit and subject to wartime mobilization. The KPA primarily fields legacy equipment, either produced in, or based on designs of, the Soviet Union and China dating back to the 1950s, 1960s, and 1970s. Although a few weapons systems are based on modern technology, the KPA has not kept pace with regional military capability developments.

...WITH EMERGING CAPABILITIES

During military parades held in Pyongyang over the last three years, many new weapon systems were displayed for the first time, highlighting continued efforts to improve the military's conventional capabilities despite financial hardships.

Ground. The parades featured several newly identified North Korean equipment, including tanks, artillery, and other armored vehicles. New infantry weapons were also revealed. The display of these systems shows that North Korea continues to produce, or at least upgrade, limited types and numbers of equipment.

Air and Air Defense. The North Korean Air Force (NKAF) operates a fleet of more than 1,300 aircraft, primarily legacy Soviet models. The NKAF's most capable combat aircraft are its MiG-29s, procured from the Soviet Union in the late 1980s. North Korea's most recent aircraft acquisition was in 1999 when it surreptitiously purchased used MiG-21s from Kazakhstan.

As the NKAF's aircraft continue to age, it increasingly relies on its ground-based air defenses and on hiding or hardening of assets to counter air attacks. During a 2010 military parade, North Korea displayed a new vertical launched mobile surface-to-air missile (SAM) launcher and accompanying radar. It bore external resemblance to the Russian S-300 and Chinese HQ-9.

North Korea publicized a March 2013 military live-fire drill that for the first time featured an unmanned aerial vehicle (UAV) in flight. The drone appeared to be a North Korean copy of a Raytheon MQM-107 Streaker target drone. North Korean press coverage of the event described the UAV as being capable of precision strike by crashing into the target. The drill also featured the UAV as a cruise-missile simulator, which was then shot down by a mobile SAM.

Naval. The North Korean Navy (NKN) has displayed limited modernization efforts, highlighted by upgrades to select surface ships and a continued program to construct small submarines. The submarine force, unsophisticated but durable, demonstrated its capabilities in March 2010 when it covertly attacked and sank the ROK warship *CHEONAN* with an indigenously produced submarine and torpedo.

Special Operations. In addition to the SOF wartime mission of deep-strike infiltrations in a combined arms peninsular attack, North Korea could also use its SOF in an asymmetric attack for political aims.

Ballistic Missile Force. North Korea has an ambitious ballistic missile development program and has deployed mobile theater ballistic missiles capable of reaching targets throughout the ROK, Japan, and the Pacific theater. Since early 2012, North Korea has made efforts to raise the public profile of its ballistic missile command, now called the Strategic Rocket Forces (SRF). Kim Jong Un's reference to the SRF during an April 15, 2012 speech seemed to elevate the command to a status on par with the Navy and Air Force. During heightened tensions on the Korean Peninsula In March 2013, North Korea made the SRF the focus of its threat to launch a nuclear attack on U.S. and ROK targets. The targets included the U.S. mainland, Hawaii, Guam, U.S. bases in the ROK, and the ROK President's residence.

North Korea displayed what it refers to as Hwasong-13 missiles, which appear to be intercontinental ballistic missiles (ICBMs),

on six road-mobile transporter-erector-launchers (TELs) during military parades in 2012 and 2013. If successfully designed and developed, the Hwasong-13 likely would be capable of reaching much of the continental United States, assuming the missiles displayed are generally representative of missiles that will be fielded. However, ICBMs are extremely complex systems that require multiple flight tests to identify and correct design or manufacturing defects, and the Hwasong-13 has not been flight-tested. Without flight tests, its current reliability as a weapon system would be low.

North Korea continues to develop the TD-2, which could reach the United States if configured as an ICBM. In April and December 2012, North Korea conducted launches of the TD-2 configured as a Space-Launch Vehicle (SLV). The April launch was a failure but the December launch was a success.

Developing an SLV contributes heavily to North Korea's long-range ballistic missile development, since the two vehicles have many shared technologies. However, a space launch does not test a reentry vehicle (RV). Without an RV capable of surviving atmospheric reentry, North Korea cannot deliver a weapon to target from an ICBM.

North Korea showcases its ballistic missile force in high-level national celebrations. Most of North Korea's ballistic missiles were paraded in July 2013. In addition to the Hwasong-13, they unveiled an intermediate-range ballistic missile (IRBM) and a version of the No Dong medium-range ballistic missile (MRBM) fitted with a cone-cylinder-flare payload at parades during the last three years. To date, the IRBM, like the new mobile ICBM, has not been flight-tested and its current reliability as a weapon system would be low. Development also continues on a solid-propellant short-range ballistic missile (SRBM).

Advances in ballistic missile delivery systems, coupled with developments in nuclear technology discussed in Chapter 5, are in line with North Korea's stated objective of being able to strike the U.S. homeland. North Korea followed its February 12, 2013 nuclear test with a campaign of media releases and authoritative public announcements reaffirming its need to counter perceived U.S. hostility with nuclear-armed ICBMs. North Korea continues to devote scarce resources to these programs, but the pace of its progress will also depend, in part, on how much technology and other aid it can gain from other countries.

__Cyberwarfare Capabilities.__ North Korea probably has a military offensive cyber operations (OCO) capability. Implicated in malicious cyber activity and cyber effects operations since 2009, North Korea may view OCO as an appealing platform from which to collect intelligence and cause disruption in South Korea.

- From 2009 to 2011, North Korea was allegedly responsible for a series of distributed denial of service attacks against South Korean commercial, government, and military websites, rendering them briefly inaccessible.
- North Korea was allegedly behind two separate cyberattacks in 2013, which targeted South Korean banking, media, and governmental networks, resulting in the erasure of critical data.

Given North Korea's bleak economic outlook, OCO may be seen as a cost-effective way to develop asymmetric, deniable military options. Because of North Korea's historical isolation from outside communications and influence, it is also likely to use Internet infrastructure from third-party nations. This increases the risk of destabilizing actions and escalation on and beyond the Korean Peninsula.

CHAPTER FOUR:
SIZE, LOCATION, AND CAPABILITIES OF NORTH KOREAN MILITARY FORCES

The KPA is a large ground force-centric military, supported by a large ballistic missile arsenal, extensive SOF, and smaller air and naval forces. With approximately 70 percent of its ground forces and 50 percent of its air and naval forces deployed within 100 kilometers of the DMZ, which has served as the de facto shared border since 1953, the KPA poses a continuous threat to the ROK and deployed U.S. forces. However, after decades under a failed economy and resulting food shortages, the KPA is a weakened force that suffers from logistical shortages, aging equipment, and inadequate training.

Ground Forces. The KPA's ground forces are dominated by regular and light infantry units, supported by armor and mechanized units and heavy concentrations of artillery. These forces are forward-deployed, fortified in several thousand underground facilities, and include long-range cannon and rocket artillery able to fire deep into the ROK, from the DMZ to Seoul, from their garrisons.

The ground forces possess numerous light and medium tanks, and many armored personnel carriers. The KPA's large artillery force includes long-range 170-mm guns and 240-mm multiple rocket launchers (MRLs), many of which are deployed along the DMZ and pose a constant threat to northern parts of the ROK, including its capital city, Seoul.

Air Forces. The Air Force is primarily responsible for defending North Korean air space. Its other missions include SOF insertion, transportation and logistics support, reconnaissance, and bombing and tactical air support for KPA ground forces. However, because of the technological inferiority of most of its aircraft fleet and rigid air defense command and control structure, much of North Korea's air defense is provided by SAMs and antiaircraft artillery (AAA).

The NKAF's most capable combat aircraft are its MiG-29 and MiG-23 fighters, and its SU-25 ground-attack aircraft. However, the majority of aircraft are less capable MiG-15s, MiG-17s, MiG-19s (F-6), and MiG-21s. The NKAF operates a large fleet of AN-2 COLT aircraft, which are 1940s vintage single-engine, 10-passenger, biplanes, likely tasked with inserting SOF into the ROK. The air force is rounded out with several hundred helicopters, predominantly Mi-2/HOPLITE and U.S.-made MD-500 helicopters obtained by circumventing

U.S. export controls in 1985. The rotary-wing fleet is used for troop transport and ground attack.

North Korea possesses a dense, overlapping air defense system of SA-2, SA-3, and SA-5 SAM sites, mobile SA-13 SAMs, mobile and fixed anti-aircraft artillery (AAA), and numerous man-portable air-defense systems like the SA-7.

Naval Forces. The North Korean Navy (NKN) is the smallest of the KPA's three main services. This coastal force is composed primarily of aging, though numerous, small patrol craft that carry a variety of anti-ship cruise missiles, torpedoes, and guns. The NKN maintains one of the world's largest submarine forces, with around 70 attack-, coastal-, and midget-type submarines. In addition, the NKN operates a large fleet of air-cushioned hovercraft and conventional landing craft to support amphibious operations and SOF insertion. The force is divided into East and West Coast Fleets, which each operate a range of patrol craft, guided-missile patrol boats, submarines, and landing craft.

Special Operations Forces. North Korean SOF are among the most highly trained, well-equipped, best-fed, and highly motivated forces in the KPA. As North Korea's conventional capabilities decline relative to the ROK and United States, North Korea appears to increasingly regard SOF capabilities as vital for asymmetric coercion.

Strategic SOF units dispersed across North Korea appear designed for rapid offensive operations, internal defense against foreign attacks, or limited attacks against vulnerable targets in the ROK as part of a coercive diplomacy effort. SOF operate in specialized units to include reconnaissance, airborne and seaborne insertion, commandos, and other specialties. All emphasize speed of movement and surprise attack to accomplish their missions. SOF may be airlifted by AN-2 COLT or helicopters (and possibly Civil Air Administration transports), moved by maritime insertion platforms, and on foot over land or via suspected underground, cross-border tunnels to attack high-value targets like command and control nodes or air bases.

Theater Ballistic Missiles. North Korea has several hundred Toksa, SCUD SRBM and No Dong MRBM missiles available for use against targets on the Korean Peninsula and Japan. The developmental IRBM, though untested and unreliable as a weapon, could also be launched at targets in the region.

Intelligence Services. North Korea leverages information collected by four intelligence organizations to plan and formulate internal policy and to undermine the political stability of South Korea. North Korean intelligence and security services collect political, military, economic, and technical information through open-source, human intelligence, and signals intelligence capabilities. North Korea's primary intelligence collection targets are South Korea, the United States, and Japan.

The Ministry of State Security (MSS) is North Korea's primary counterintelligence service and is an autonomous agency of the North Korean government reporting directly to Kim Jong Un. The MSS is responsible for operating North Korean prison camps, investigating cases of domestic espionage, repatriating defectors, and conducting overseas counterespionage activities.

The United Front Department (UFD) overtly attempts to establish pro-North Korean groups in South Korea such as the Korean Asia-Pacific Committee and the Ethnic Reconciliation Council. The UFD is also the primary department involved in managing inter-Korean dialogue and North Korea's policy toward the South.

North Korea's Reconnaissance General Bureau (RGB) is responsible for clandestine operations. The RGB includes six bureaus charged with operations, reconnaissance, technology and cyber, overseas intelligence, inter-Korean talks, and service support.

The 225th Bureau is responsible for training agents, infiltrating South Korea, and establishing underground political parties focused on fomenting unrest and revolution.

Command and Control. The DPRK National Defense Commission (NDC) is the symbolic nominal authority over the North's military and security services. The Ministry of Peoples Armed Forces (MPAF) is the administrative superior of the KPA, while operational command and control is exercised by its subordinate General Staff Department. The 1992 constitution gives control of the North's military to the NDC, and Kim Jong Un exercises control of the military as "first chairman" of the NDC and supreme commander of the KPA. Kim Jong Un further exercises control as first secretary of the Korean Worker's Party (KWP) and chairman of the KWP's Central Military Commission.

Telecommunications. North Korea has a nationwide fiber-optic network, and has invested in a modern nationwide cellular network. However, telecommunication services and access are strictly controlled, and all networks are available for military use, if necessary.

Cell phone subscribership increased beyond 2 million with the growth of Koryolink, North Korea's 3G cellular network. Mobile phone users consist primarily of high-ranking officials in Pyongyang and their families, though ownership is beginning to spread into smaller cities and towns. Most cell phones cannot access the Internet and can only make calls within North Korea.

North Koreans are restricted from using the Internet, but are able to access the national intranet, which is insulated from the World Wide Web. The intranet hosts government-approved websites, including Korean Central News Agency and North Korean propaganda website Uriminzokkiri.

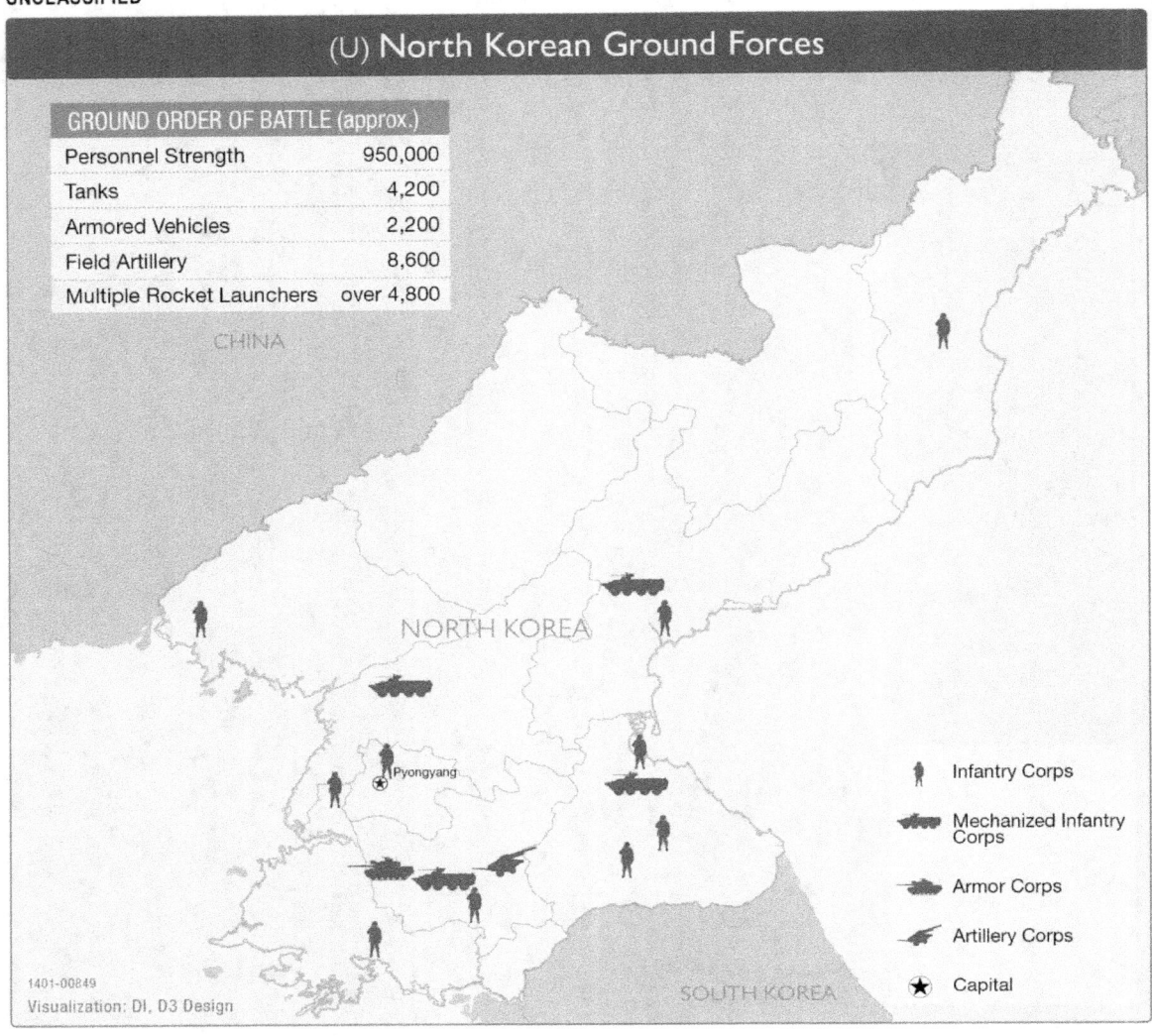

(U) North Korean Ground Forces

GROUND ORDER OF BATTLE (approx.)	
Personnel Strength	950,000
Tanks	4,200
Armored Vehicles	2,200
Field Artillery	8,600
Multiple Rocket Launchers	over 4,800

CHINA

NORTH KOREA

Pyongyang

SOUTH KOREA

Infantry Corps

Mechanized Infantry Corps

Armor Corps

Artillery Corps

Capital

1401-00849
Visualization: DI, D3 Design

(U) North Korean Air Forces

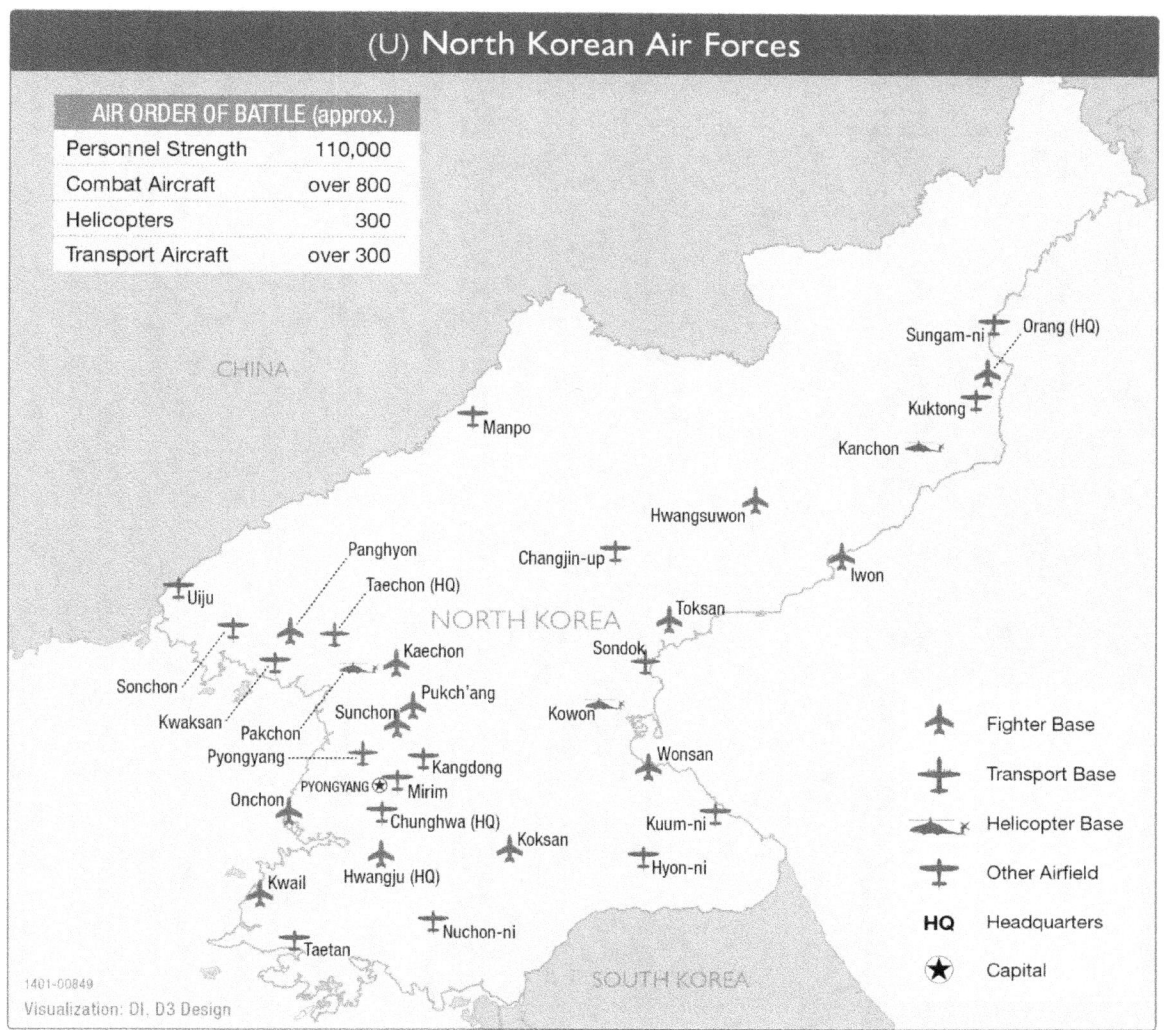

AIR ORDER OF BATTLE (approx.)

Personnel Strength	110,000
Combat Aircraft	over 800
Helicopters	300
Transport Aircraft	over 300

Legend:
- Fighter Base
- Transport Base
- Helicopter Base
- Other Airfield
- **HQ** Headquarters
- Capital

1401-00849
Visualization: DI, D3 Design

(U) North Korean Naval Forces

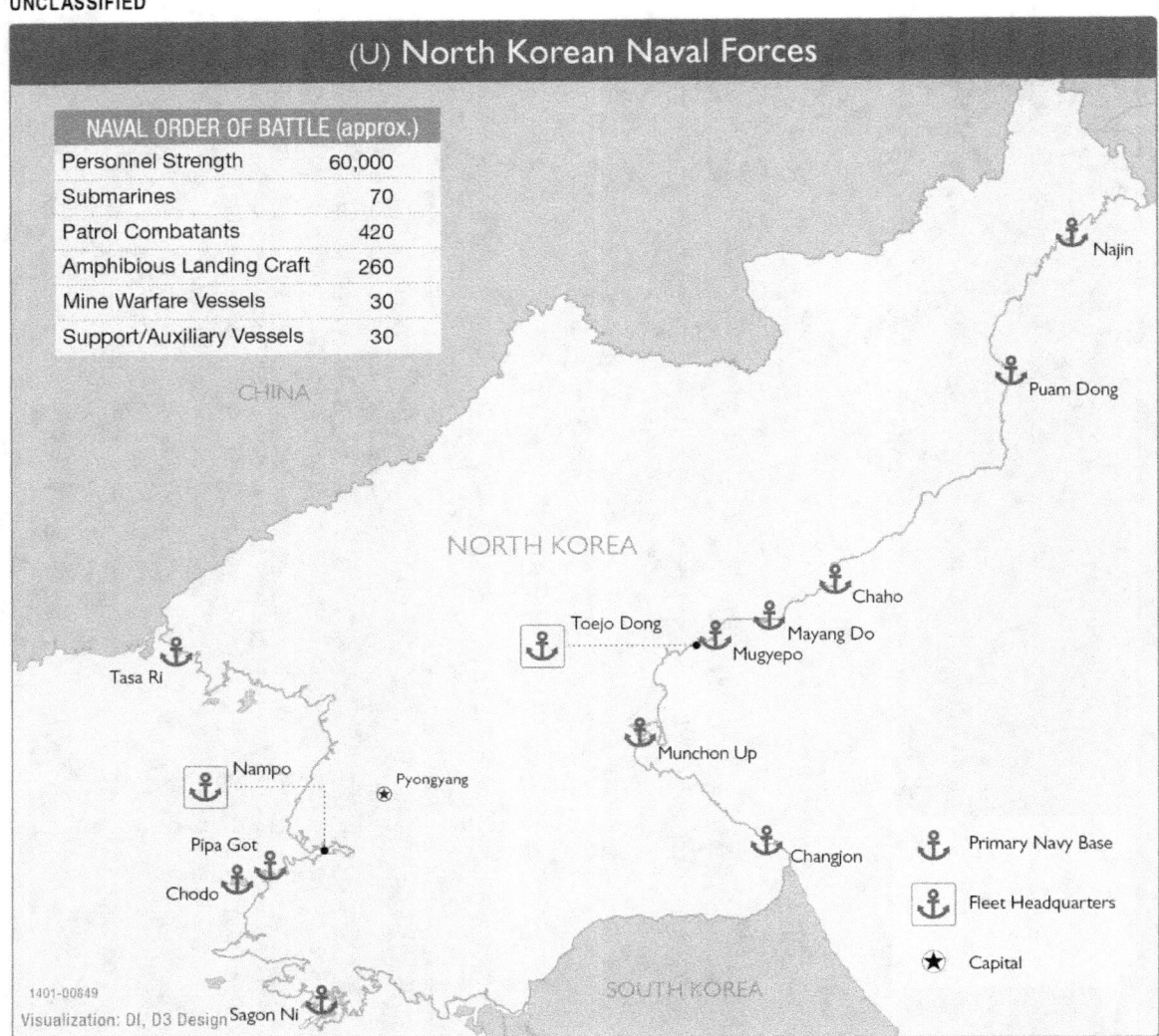

NAVAL ORDER OF BATTLE (approx.)	
Personnel Strength	60,000
Submarines	70
Patrol Combatants	420
Amphibious Landing Craft	260
Mine Warfare Vessels	30
Support/Auxiliary Vessels	30

CHINA

NORTH KOREA

Najin

Puam Dong

Chaho

Toejo Dong

Mayang Do

Mugyepo

Tasa Ri

Munchon Up

Nampo

Pyongyang

Pipa Got

Changjon

Chodo

Sagon Ni

Primary Navy Base

Fleet Headquarters

Capital

SOUTH KOREA

1401-00849

Visualization: DI, D3 Design

North Korean Ballistic Missile Forces

System	Launchers	Estimated Range
Toksa	Fewer than 100	75 miles
SCUD-B		185 miles
SCUD-C		310 miles
SCUD-ER		435-625 miles
No Dong	Fewer than 50	800 miles
IRBM	Fewer than 50	2,000+ miles
TD-2	Unknown*	3,400+ miles
Hwasong-13 (Road-Mobile ICBM)	At least 6	3,400+ miles

Note: North Korea has an ambitious ballistic missile development program and has exported missile technology to other countries, including Iran and Pakistan. North Korea has produced its own version of the SCUD B, and the SCUD C, an extended-range version of the SCUD B. North Korea will continue using and improving the TD-2, which could reach the United States with a nuclear payload if developed as an ICBM. North Korea is also developing the Hwasong-13, which appears to be a road-mobile ICBM, and has twice paraded six launchers for the system. The Hwasong-13 and an IRBM have not been flight-tested and their current reliability as weapon systems would be low. A short-range, solid-propellant ballistic missile is also being developed.

* Launches of the TD-2 have been observed from both east and west coast launch facilities.

CHAPTER FIVE: PROLIFERATION

OVERVIEW

North Korea has been an exporter of conventional arms and ballistic missiles for several decades. Despite the adoption of United Nations Security Council resolutions (UNSCRs) 1718, 1874, 2087, and 2094, which prohibit all weapons sales and the provision of related technical training from North Korea, the DPRK continues to market, sell, and deliver weapons-related goods and services. Weapons sales are a critical source of foreign currency for North Korea, which is unlikely to cease export activity in spite of UN Security Council sanctions or increased international efforts to interdict its weapons-related exports.

CONVENTIONAL ARMS AND MISSILE SALES

North Korea uses a worldwide network to facilitate arms sales activities and maintains a core, but dwindling group of recipient countries including Iran, Syria, and Burma. North Korea has exported conventional and ballistic missile-related equipment, components, materials, and technical assistance to countries in Africa, Asia, and the Middle East. Conventional weapons sales have included ammunition, small arms, artillery, armored vehicles, and surface-to-air missiles.

- In addition to Iran and Syria, past clients for North Korea's ballistic missiles and associated technology have included Egypt, Iraq, Libya, Pakistan, and Yemen. Burma has begun distancing itself from North Korea but remains a conventional weapons customer.

North Korea uses various methods to circumvent UNSCRs, including falsifying end-user certificates, mislabeling crates, sending cargo through multiple front companies and intermediaries, and using air cargo for deliveries of high-value and sensitive arms exports.

NUCLEAR PROLIFERATION

One of our gravest concerns about North Korea's activities in the international arena is its demonstrated willingness to proliferate nuclear technology. North Korea provided Libya with uranium hexafluoride, the form of uranium used in the uranium enrichment process to produce fuel for nuclear reactors and nuclear weapons, via the proliferation network of Pakistani nuclear scientist AQ Khan. North Korea also provided Syria with nuclear reactor technology until 2007.

NORTH KOREA'S WMD PROGRAMS

Nuclear Weapons. North Korea conducted nuclear tests in 2006, 2009, and most recently in February 2013.

North Korea continues to invest in its nuclear infrastructure and could conduct additional nuclear tests at any time. In 2010, North Korea revealed a uranium enrichment facility at Yongbyon that it claims is for producing fuel for a light water reactor under construction. In April 2013, North Korea announced its intent to restart and refurbish the nuclear facilities at Yongbyon, including this enrichment facility and the nuclear reactor that had been shut down since 2007. Press reports from September and October 2013 claim the reactor has been restarted and is once again operating.

These activities violate North Korea's obligations under UNSCRs 1718, 1874, 2087, and 2094, contravene its commitments under the September 19, 2005 Joint Statement of the Six-Party Talks, and increase the risk of proliferation.

Biological Weapons. Although North Korea is a party to the Biological and Toxic Weapons Convention, open sources have often reported defector allegations of a North Korean biological warfare program. These sources indicate that North Korea continues to research bacterial and viral biological agents that could support an offensive biological weapons program. Its existing research infrastructure, combined with its weapons industry, gives North Korea a potentially robust biological warfare capability.

Chemical Weapons. North Korea probably has had a longstanding chemical weapons (CW) program with the capability to produce nerve, blister, blood, and choking agents and likely possesses a CW stockpile. North Korea probably could employ CW agents by modifying a variety of conventional munitions, including artillery and ballistic missiles. In addition, North Korean forces are prepared to operate in a contaminated environment; they train regularly in chemical defense operations. North Korea is not a party to the Chemical Weapons Convention.

INTERDICTED TRANSFERS

Global concern about North Korea's proliferation activity continues to mount, leading various nations to take action. Notable recent interdiction events pursuant to UNSCRs include:

- In early July 2013, Panamanian authorities stopped and inspected the North Korean flagged vessel Chong Chon Gang, finding hidden cargo including two MiG-21 fighter aircraft and associated engines, SA-2 and SA-3 SAM-related equipment, and unspecified missiles. Cuba issued a statement acknowledging ownership of the military equipment and claiming it was being sent to North Korea for overhaul.

- In June 2011, the M/V Light, a vessel bound for Burma suspected of carrying military-related cargo, returned to North Korea after refusing a U.S. Navy inspection request.

- In February 2010, South Africa seized North Korean-origin spare tank parts destined for the Republic of Congo.

- In December 2009, Thai authorities impounded the cargo of a chartered cargo plane containing about 35 metric tons of North Korean weapons, including artillery rockets, rocket-propelled grenades, and SAMs.

- In October 2009, the ROK seized North Korean-origin chemical warfare protective suits destined for Syria.

Although some of its weapons-transfer attempts have been interdicted by the international community, North Korea will continue to attempt arms shipments via new and increasingly complex routes.